The poem for our world

Ryann Lightfoot

Presentation by *BookLeaf Publishing*

Web: www.bookleafpub.com

E-mail: info@bookleafpub.com

ISBN: 9789395620154

First edition 2022

The room I dance

In the small room, I dance.
In the fancy room, I twirl.
I feel happy.
I fell lightly, I jumped so high, that some even
say I can fly.
I dance with patients, and I dance as my hair
covers my face.
I touch the roof and think to myself it's my
favorite place.

me and a Best friend

On a sunny day me and my dog play.
We run across the road so fast the wind goes
cold.
I toss the ball at my best friend, he runs, he
gallops, he paints.
Me and him play till the day ends, well until our
mother calls us in.

Why can't I see stars in the day?

why can't I see stars in the day such a beautiful
thing, to light up the night sky but disappear in
the day?
Why can't I see stars in the day? "All great
things have to go away", my mother tells me as
the sun comes up and the stars slowly fade away.
Why can't I see stars in the day, I will wait till
the sun goes down and they come from the
clouds.

who names the months?

Who names the months of the year?
was it meant to be a joke?
when I think of this question I think of a group
of old folk. Was it just one morning they
thought these months needed a name?
"your name will be April and you June" Was this
man insane?!
Who named the months, what a crazy thing, and
don't even get me started on the days of the
week!

Coach

A coach what a funny thing.

A coach is one of the more spiller things.

A coach old or new there's not much to it.

A coach is not a bed but the next best thing to it.

Oh but a coach is such a silly thing.

The sound of the class room

The clicking of the pen, as I watch my teacher
cringe.
The talking of the kids as the teacher pauses and
waits for the speaking to end.
The sound of the soft music as the children
whisper softer.
The big windows show the still playground.
 As the pencil hits the paper. As the children
laugh
and the music that plays so soft non of us can
hear. At this time it hits me it's going to be a
long year.

Right before school

Getting out of bed. dreams flying through my head, walking down the stairs. still needing to fix my hair, slowly making my bed. knowing it will get messed up by the end. putting on my shoes, lines still on my face, the bedtime bruise. The walk to the bus stop not, a run or a hop. The kids on the bus screamed it was quiet in my dream. got out of bed dreams still nestled in my head. I close my eyes and hope it wouldn't be a long ride.

pretty little flower

As pretty as a flower.
Soft as silk.
Bright as day.
But still as dull as gray.
As loud as an alarm.
But as quiet as a mouse.
As pretty as a flower.
and as soft as the music that plays in my house.

Morning rush

In the morning I'm truly in a rush, grab my shoes
can't miss the bus.
still need to brush my teeth let's hope no one is
next to me. in the mornings I really am in a rush
out the door and I grab my lunch. my mom is
still asleep, I walk past her room and hear her
say what a week. In the mornings I'm in such a
rush but it wasn't me who missed the bus, turned
out today was Sunday funny thing I did the same
thing yesterday!

The colors of the town

The colors of my small town, I see all around.
Blue like the sky.
Green like the trees.
And black like the street I help the old lady
across.
Also Yellow like the bus.
 I love the colors of my street.

New girl

There is a new girl in class, it's hard not to stare.
I look at her she's thinking so she does not care.
I don't know her maybe we could be friends by
the end of the year.

Forever

cold or warm.
Happy or sad.
Night or day.
In my bed, I will forever stay.

Make my day

13

Sweet, grandmas lips or... like
the candy we sneak.
Pink, nails or... like my stuff animal snake.
My favorite things always make my day.

Season

The cold winter days.
The hot summer evening.
The windy nights.
I wake up and freeze, and play in the sun and
hear the sound of the wind as I run.
The cold days, hot evenings, and windy nights.

Colors special to me

Red like lips when grandma gives me a kiss.
yellow like the sun, after school I stop by the
pool. blue like water oh I hope it doesn't get any
hotter. Orange my tree waves in the wind to me.
or white like the clouds as puffy as my hair.
but most of all brown-like skin that glistens in
the sun.

What I see

A bridge, a pound, and a tree is what I see. A
bridge, a lake, and a tree were all here before
me. A frog, a bird the wind, is what I hear. A
frog, a bird the wind, were the only things I hear.

The man that lives in the attic

The man living in the attic only comes out at
night.
The man in the attic also likes to hide.
The tiptoe he thinks we can't hear.
the squeaking of our old house stares.
 The shaping of the latches the clicking of the
key.
But in the middle of the night, I see the man
from the attack looking at me.

night

It's a gloomy night, but I see the light from the
fireflies as they glide by.
I notice a dog at play. my mother walks in to say
good night, I close my eyes and wait for day.
when the sunrise it will be me at play.

www.ingramcontent.com/pod-product-compliance
Lightning Source LLC
Chambersburg PA
CBHW061326140726
47998CB00007B/2572